Beginning composition t

J B Heaton

Illustrations by James Moss

Longman

LONGMAN GROUP UK LIMITED
Longman House, Burnt Mill
Harlow, Essex CM20 2JE, England
and Associated Companies throughout the world.

First published 1975
Twenty-third impression 1990

Produced by Longman Group (FE) Ltd
Printed in Hong Kong

ISBN 0-582-55519-1

Contents

Foreword to the teacher

Beginning Composition through Pictures has been written for pupils who have been learning English as a second or foreign language for only two or three years. A selection of basic sentence patterns and grammatical items is given for each picture composition. The first few compositions, for example, deal with such items as *There are*, the present continuous tense, the position of adjectives, simple spatial prepositions, *can*, the present simple tense with *want* and *like*, etc. Later such items as *When* clauses, *has to, too small to* are practised.

Pictures can be of great help in the teaching of new vocabulary and structures by providing the pupil with the basic ideas and material for his composition. The pupil's attention can be drawn by visual means to significant detail and to the more relevant aspects of each composition. At the same time, his imagination is also stimulated.

The basic vocabulary is controlled to a large extent for each picture, though each situation, itself, must largely influence the choice of vocabulary presented. The situation is thus of the utmost relevance in determining the selection of vocabulary required for communication. Sometimes new words not required in the pupil's active vocabulary may be required for a particular composition. All such words are both illustrated in the pictures and listed below the pictures. Key words, including new or difficult words, are included in the lists, and may help to spark off ideas about the pictures. Also included in the lists are a few words required for the sentence table rather than for the composition. Usually, more words are given in each list than strictly necessary in order to allow for a choice of words by the pupils. The dialogue following the list of key words should be thoroughly practised before any written work from the sentence table is attempted. It is advisable for pupils to memorise one of the conversations. However, they should be encouraged to speak naturally to the pupils they are addressing. In other words, they should be required to speak as if they were engaged in a normal conversation in pairs or in small groups. Several pairs or groups of pupils can practise the conversation at the same time if they turn round to face one another. The teacher can then walk round the class, correcting individual pupils. Later, a few students can be asked to speak and act the conversation at the front of the class while the other pupils watch and listen.

The following steps are suggested for teaching conversations:

1 The pupils look at the appropriate picture(s) while the teacher explains the situation for the dialogue. E.g. (Picture Composition

10) 'David is trying hard to row his boat to the shore, but he doesn't know how to row. Look at his father in Picture 1. His father's name is Mr Black. Mr Black is angry with David because David cannot row.' Etc.

2 The teacher reads the conversation to the pupils. He tries to speak naturally (without undue stress or exaggeration).

3 The teacher then asks a few simple questions to make sure that the pupils know what the conversation is all about. 'Who is rowing the boat?' 'Who is on the shore?' 'Why can't David reach the shore?' Etc.

4 The pupils then repeat each line of the dialogue after the teacher. The teacher stops at the end of each line to give the pupils an opportunity to repeat it, taking care to correct errors of pronunciation, stress and intonation.

5 The class are divided into two sections, each section taking the part of one of the speakers in the dialogue. (The teacher is advised to put the dialogue on the board and to rub out words and phrases as the class proceed to memorise the dialogue.)

6 Pairs or small groups of pupils may then say the dialogue to each other, using simple gestures.

7 A few pupils are chosen to act the dialogues at the front of the class. The class may look at either the pupils or the pictures in their books.

Each sentence pattern or grammatical item included in a sentence table should also be practised orally before the pupil begins the written work involved in this exercise. Further opportunity for the item to be used is provided in the questions in Exercise 4, and the teacher should later encourage the pupil to use the item in his composition work in Exercise 6.

The aim of introducing and practising important words and structures as previously outlined is to give the pupil a thorough preparation for the composition work. The importance of a thorough preparation for both oral and written composition cannot be too greatly stressed at this stage. Generally, the teacher is advised to complete the oral preparation and questions before beginning any written work (although this rule is not, of course, an inflexible one).
Each composition may be treated as primarily oral or as primarily written. Further preparatory exercises to the ones given may be organised in a number of different ways. If he considers that the class requires additional preparation, the teacher may care to introduce the

Look and Point method. For example, *before* asking the ten questions about Picture Composition 1, he may ask the pupils to look and point to the man running to catch the train, the two men drinking tea, the guard holding the flag, etc. Alternatively, *after* asking questions about Picture Composition 5, he may wish to read out four sentences, each describing one of the pictures in the story. Thus, he may say: 'The woman is bringing the man a cup of tea' or 'The boy is lying down to paint', etc. and he will ask the class to look at and point to the appropriate picture.

Additional written work may be set either as further preparation for composition writing or else as follow-up work. Here are some examples of just a few of the different types of written exercises which may be set in addition to Exercise 5:

1 Vocabulary (Picture Composition 1) Choose the correct word from the brackets: A man is hurrying past the (engine driver, ticket collector, guard). He is trying to (mount, get, catch) a train.

2 Adjectives (Picture Composition 8) A (strong, light, warm) wind has torn the sails.

3 Prepositions (Picture Composition 16) There is a post office (behind, opposite, at the side of) the stalls.

4 Verbs (Picture Composition 24) Put the verbs into the correct tense form. Write the story in the past and make any changes which are necessary: The train (stop) and the children (tell) the engine driver about the landslide. 'There (be) a landslide,' they (tell) him.

5 Articles (Picture Composition 16) Bob and Tina are looking at _____map of_____city. They stop and ask_____policeman_____ way.

Additional preparatory work may be done for the composition in any of the following ways. In certain instances the teacher may even wish to devise such exercises as the following to replace the free written work or to support the writing exercise given before each composition.

1 Completion (a) (Picture Composition 2) Complete the following story by adding one word in each blank.
A boy is playing with his_____. He is showing it to his friend. 'My dog is very_____,' he says. He is throwing an old_____ and his dog is_____after it.
(b) (Picture Composition 8) Complete the following sentences by adding as many words as you like.

Dave and Tom are sailing in a small boat when_____
_____

They are very frightened but _____
_____

2 Multiple Choice (Picture Composition 22) Write out this story. Choose the best word.
Dave put on his (a) clothes (b) swimming trunks (c) trousers and ran to the (a) lake (b) river (c) sea. The tide came in quickly and reached the rock, so Dave got out of the sea and ran to (a) his clothes (b) the street (c) a race.

3 Joining Sentences (Picture Composition 25) Join the correct parts and write out the complete sentence. (Each part should be used once only.)

Three small boys	had a puncture.
Four big boys pushed	wait for the next bus.
They got on the bus	passed the 26 bus.
The small boys had to	were waiting for a bus.
After half an hour	but the small boys could not get on.
The 26 bus	they got on a 33 bus.
The 33 bus	in front of the small boys.

4 Rearranging sentences (Picture Composition 13) Put these sentences in the right order.
It was Mr Gregg!
A head suddenly appeared at the window.
The boy picked up a newspaper to hit the fly.
He missed it and became angry.
A boy and girl and their parents were eating but a fly disturbed them.
The fly then landed on something outside the window.
This time the boy tried to hit it very hard.

Other exercises may be introduced to bring in imaginary conversations between the people in a picture. The pupil may also be given simple comprehension questions on the contents of a picture. Although the teacher may make unlimited use of the pictures for language work, he should never lose sight of the fact that each picture or series of pictures is designed chiefly for one purpose—the teaching of composition. Exercises are generally useful only to the extent that they are directly related to the composition work. In addition to the picture stories, this book also includes a few pictures for description and for comparison as well as maps and plans for instructions and description.

The appendix contains a list of the chief structures and also helpful phrases for describing the pictures. Some teachers may prefer their pupils not to use this section at all. The pupil should spend a few minutes looking at each picture or set of pictures before the teacher asks questions about them. He should be told to listen very carefully to the teacher and to watch the teacher's lips as he asks each question. Throughout the book, Exercise 6 may be given as an oral composition or as a written composition. Pupils must be encouraged and helped to make the characters in each story real and alive: for this reason particularly, they should be instructed to give a name to each character. The naming of characters is an important step towards visualisation and identification. Finally, it is important that students attempt Exercise 6 (Composition) without referring back to Exercise 5, thereby avoiding the temptation to copy the phrases and sentences in this exercise. It is hoped that he will find the compositions varied and interesting.

1 A busy railway station

1

railway station, platform, guard, ticket collector, flag, whistle, passengers, restaurant, suitcase, entrance; hurry, approach; late

2

Ticket Collector	Are you catching this train, sir?
Mr Watson	Yes, I am.
Ticket Collector	Please hurry along.
Mr Watson	But I *am* hurrying.
Policeman	What's the matter?
Tom	I'm waiting for my mother.
Policeman	Where is she?
Tom	She's buying a ticket, but she's a long time.

3

Use the sentence table to write two correct sentences about the picture:

There is	a	train taxi boy policeman	in the station outside the entrance on the platform
There are	two some a lot of	buses men trains people	near the restaurant on the train

Now write two correct sentences from the following table:

A	policeman man	is	hurrying past the ticket collector approaching the little boy
Some	men people	are	leaving the train drinking tea

4

a Is Mr Watson walking or running?
b What's he doing?
c What time is it?
d At what time does the train leave?
e What's the guard doing?
f Is the other train arriving or leaving?
g What's there outside the station?
h What's there near the two men outside the restaurant?

i Where's the little boy sitting?
j Who is approaching him?

5

Write out the following paragraph. Choose the correct words:

There are two trains on the platform. Some people are opening
They   in the station.   is

the doors of one of the trains and get off. A man is hurrying
                                      getting off.

past the platform. He wants to ride the train to
         ticket collector.   catch

Greenfields and he is running towards it. The clock is 8.54 and
           but   time

the train arrives at 8.55. It There is a small boy on the platform.
          leaves

There is sitting on a large suitcase and but he is crying. A policeman is
He   at   but

arriving him. There are two men and woman near the restaurant.
approaching   a woman

The two men are drinking tea and talking to a the woman.
                          the tea   the

6

Now write a few sentences of your own about this picture.

2 A clever dog

1

dog, shoe, basket, tin can, bush; clever, proud, angry, surprised; throw, appear

2

Bill	Watch Toby. He's very clever.
Harry	He's a silly dog.
Bill	No, he isn't. Watch him.
Harry	What are you doing with that old shoe?

Bill	Look, Toby's bringing back the shoe.
Harry	He *is* clever.
Bill	Oh dear! This is a new shoe.
Harry	And look at that man. Why is he angry with us?
Bill	It's *his* shoe!

3

Use the sentence table to write two correct sentences about the pictures:

	an old		
Bill is throwing away His dog is bringing back	a	small new different	tin can shoe

Now write two correct sentences from the following table:

Bill The man	is	surprised at angry with kind to	the dog Toby
Bill and Harry are		proud of	

4

a What's Bill picking up in Picture 1?
b Where's Bill throwing the shoe?
c What's his friend doing?
d Is the dog running towards Bill or is it running after the shoe in Picture 2?
e Are the two boys following the dog or are they standing still?
f What's the dog doing in Picture 3?
g Is the shoe a new one or an old one?
h Is the man in Picture 4 angry with the dog or proud of it?
i Where's he going?
j Why are the two boys very surprised?

5

Read the following six sentences. Write them out in their correct order.

He is throwing it into some bushes.
But it is not the same shoe: it is a new shoe.
Bill is picking up an old shoe.
It belongs to a man and he is very angry with Bill and Harry.
His dog is running after it.
The dog is bringing back a shoe and Bill is very proud.

6

Now write this story in a few sentences of your own.

9

3 A 'dream' holiday

1

picture, beach, sand, sandcastle, fan, radio, noise; noisy, hot, quiet, lonely, crowded; look at, lie, sing, shout, fight

2

Bill Short	I'm tired. I need a holiday.
Alan Banks	Yes, I want one, too.
Bill Short	Where do you want to go?
Alan Banks	To the seaside, of course.

Bill Short	There are a lot of people here. It's crowded.
Mr Short	Don't you like this place?
Bill Short	I don't like crowded beaches.
Mr Short	Look! What are those boys doing over there?
Bill Short	They're fighting. It's just like school!

3

Use the sentence table to write two correct sentences about the pictures:

Bill Alan Banks	wants needs		on a quiet beach
They all Bill and Alan	want need	a holiday	near the sea

Now write two correct sentences from the following table:

Bill Short Alan	doesn't	like	a lot of noise
Bill and Alan They	don't		crowded beaches

4

a What's Bill Short looking at in Picture 1?
b Is Bill talking to Alan Banks or to the teacher?
c Does Alan Banks also want a holiday?
d Is the beach quiet or crowded in the picture in the classroom?
e Where's Bill in Picture 2?
f Is the beach crowded or is it empty?
g Who is with Bill?
h What are the people doing in the picture in the classroom?
i What are they doing in Picture 2?
j Why doesn't Bill like the beach?

5

The paragraph below is about Picture 1. Write it out and choose the best word for each number. E.g. There are a lot of *pupils* in the . . .

There are a lot of (1) in the (2). Some are playing happily but others (3). Alan and Bill are (4). The picture in the classroom shows a (5). There are only four people (6). Bill doesn't like (7). He wants a (8).

(1)	(2)	(3)
pupils	picture	are fighting
people	beach	fighting
pictures	classroom	fight

(4)	(5)	(6)
fighting	large school	in the classroom
talking	sunny beach	near the wall
studying	busy street	on the beach

(7)	(8)
a lot of noise	study
his friend	holiday
the pictures in the classroom	work

6

Now write a few sentences about Picture 2.

4 Danger on the road

1

cycle, cyclist, bell, lorry, (a) bend, accident, airfield, plane, walker;
careless, fast; travel, ring, approach, pass, crash, (to) land, take off

2

Ted Smart	Oh dear. This lorry's going very slowly.
Pete Smart	I'm going to ring my bell.
Ted Smart	Oh, I'm going to pass it.
Pete Smart	Well, I'm not going to wait. I'm going to pass it, too.

Lorry Driver	There are two cyclists behind us.
Friend	What are they doing?
Lorry Driver	They're going to pass us—and just on this bend.
Friend	They're very foolish. They'll have an accident.

3

Use the sentence table to write four correct sentences about the
pictures:

Ted Smart The lorry driver The motorcycle The plane	is going to	land pass the lorry have an accident take off
Ted and Pete The cyclists	are going to	

4

a   Is the road in the picture straight?
b   Where are the cyclists in the picture?
c   Are the two boys careful or careless?
d   What are they going to do?
e   What's going to happen?
f   What are the two men on the motorcycle looking at?
g   What's the plane going to do?
h   Who's standing behind the cycles and the lorry?
i   What's he going to do?

5

Write out the paragraph below. Put the verbs in the brackets in the
correct tense: use either *going to (do)* or *is/are (do)ing.*

There are two cyclists in the picture. They are near a lorry and
(pass) it. The lorry (travel) very slowly round a bend. A motorcycle
(approach) them round the corner, but the two boys cannot see it.
One of the men on the motorcycle (point) at a plane. The plane (land)
soon. The motorcyclist (drive) carelessly and there (be) an accident.

6

Now write this story in a few sentences of your own.

5 Wet paint

1

step-ladder, piece of wood, ceiling, wall, floor, can of paint, brush; wet (paint), lazy, happy, puzzled; lie, kneel down, enjoy, cross, reach

2

Peter	Why are you smiling, mother?
Mrs Green	Because I'm happy. You're helping your father.
Peter	We're going to paint this room very quickly.
Mrs Green	Do you want a cup of tea?
Peter	Yes, please, but we can't hold it. We've got a brush in one hand and a can of paint in the other.
Mrs Green	The room is very nice now.
Mr Green	Yes, it looks very nice indeed.
Mrs Green	But how are you going to get out of the room?
Mr Green	What do you mean? Oh dear, the paint's still wet. We can't move.

3

Find the correct answer in Table B to each question in Table A. Write out the four questions with the four answers:

A

Why	is	Mrs Green happy	?
		Peter painting the room	?
	can't	Mr Green take the cup of tea	?
		they get out of the room	?

B

Because	he wants to help his father
	the paint is still wet
	Mr Green and Peter are painting the room
	he has a brush in one hand and a can of paint in the other

Now check your answers with the following table:

Mrs Green is happy		Mr Green and Peter are painting the room
Peter is painting the room	because	he wants to help his father
Mr Green can't take the cup of tea		he has a brush in one hand and a can of paint in the other
They can't get out of the room		the paint is still wet

4

a What are Peter and his father doing in all the pictures?
b What part of the room is Peter painting in Picture 1?
c What's Mrs Green doing in this picture?
d What's she doing in Picture 2?
e Why can't Peter take the cup of tea?
f Where's Mr Green sitting in this picture?
g What part of the room are they painting in Picture 3?
h Are they happy or miserable?
i What are they looking at in Picture 4?
j What can't they do? Why not?

5

Join the correct part of the sentence in List B with each part in List A.

A

Peter's father is beginning
Peter is painting the room, too,
He is lying down on a piece of wood
Mrs Green is giving Peter and his father some tea
They cannot take the tea from her
Peter and his father are kneeling down
They are finishing painting the room
They cannot get out of the room

B

and painting the floor.
but they cannot drink it.
because there is wet paint on the floor.
and painting the ceiling.
because he wants to help his father.
and they are looking puzzled.
to paint a room.
because they are holding brushes and cans of paint.

6

Now imagine that you are the boy. You are helping your father to paint the room. Write this story in a few sentences of your own.

6 'Increase in prices'

1

store, shop, village, (a) queue, ice cream, cigar, goods, (an) increase, price, manager, shop assistant, everything; busy; (to) queue, (to) increase, go up, rise, reduce, pay for; nearby

2

Manager	Sorry. You haven't given me enough money.
Leela	I've given you six pence.
Manager	An ice cream costs eight pence.
Leela	But it only cost six pence yesterday.
Manager	There's been an increase in prices. The price of everything has gone up.
Ann	Look. There's a new shop over there. It's just opened.
Leela	Yes, and everything is cheaper.
Ann	The other shop is empty.
Leela	I'm not going to buy ice cream there again.

3

Use the sentence table to write four correct sentences about Picture 1 and two correct sentences about Picture 2:

Leela The fat man	has	just	joined the queue paid for the ice cream
Leela and Ann The children	have	already	seen another shop sat down gone to the new shop

4

a   Why are the children in Picture 1 queuing?
b   Where have they come from?
c   What have the girl and the boy just done?
d   What's the shop assistant doing?
e   Has the shop increased or reduced the prices of goods?
f   What are the men near the school doing?
g   Why aren't there any children at the shop in Picture 2?
h   What's there on the other side of the road?
i   Where are all the children?
j   Why is the fat man no longer happy?

5

Write out the following paragraph about Pictures 1 and 2. Choose the best word for each number. E.g. In Picture 1 there is a *queue* outside the shop . . .

In Picture 1 there is a (1) outside the shop. A lot of children from the (2) school are (3) things in the shop (4) it is the only shop in the village. The shop has just (5) the (6) of everything, and so the children are not happy. In Picture 2 there are two shops. Another shop has just (7) and all the children have gone there because everything is (8).

(1)	(2)	(3)	(4)
queue	nearly	paying	but
line	nearby	selling	because
row	near	buying	then

(5)	(6)	(7)	(8)
gone up	number	opened	cheaper
risen	money	begun	fewer
increased	price	built	free

6

Now write this story in a few sentences of your own.

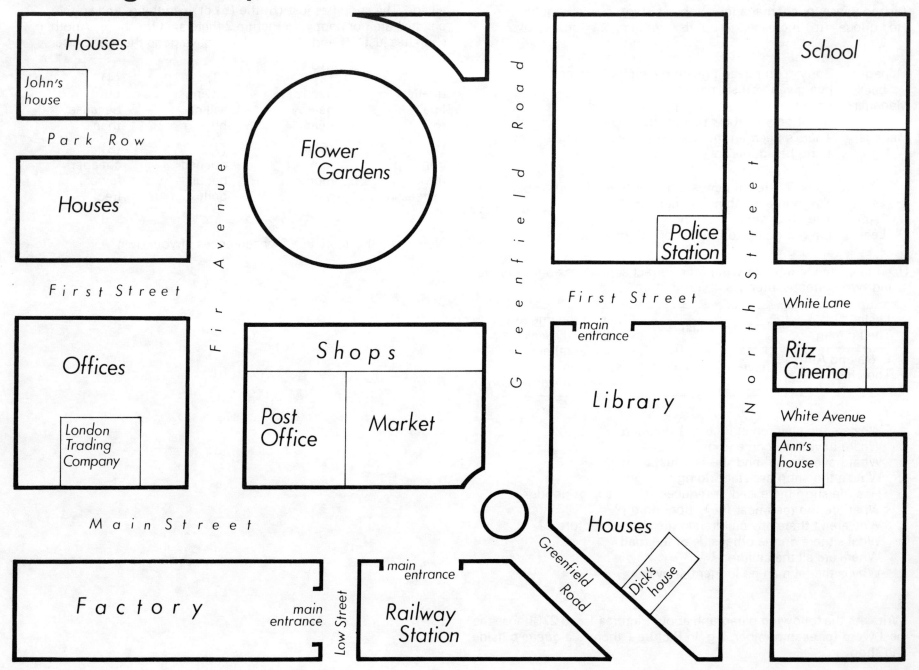

1

street, road, avenue, lane, row, crossroads, junction, roundabout, gardens, market, trade, trading company, factory, library, police-station, railway station, post office, cinema, entrance, direction; main; left, right, straight on; turn, bear, pass, run past

2

Bill	Where is the post office, please?
Ann	It's in Fir Avenue—near the flower gardens.
Bill	Are there some shops near the gardens?
Ann	That's right. The post office is at the side of the shops. There's a big market on the other side of it.

Ted	Excuse me. How can I get to the railway station from here?
Policeman	You're now at the Ritz. Go along First Street.
Ted	Where's First Street?
Policeman	It's that street over there. Go right along it to the end. Then turn left and go down Greenfield Road to the roundabout. You'll see the entrance to the station opposite you.

3

a   I am at Ann's house and I want to go to the school. Write two correct sentences from the sentence tables to tell me how to get there. (Use one sentence from each table.)

b   I am at John's house and I want to go to the factory. Write three correct sentences from the sentence tables to tell me how to get there. (Use one sentence from the first table and two sentences from the second table.)

Go straight on			crossroads
Turn	left	at the	end of the street
Bear	right		junction

			right	
The	post office	is	on the	right
	school			left
	factory		in front of you	

4

a   Is there a cinema or a factory opposite Ann's house?
b   Which road runs past the London Trading Company?
c   The library is on one side of First Street. What's on the other side?
d   Does John live near the flower gardens or does Dick live near them?
e   Are the shops near the school or near the post office?
f   Where is the post office?
g   Where is Dick's house?
h   Where does Ann live?
i   Do I go along Fir Avenue or North Street to reach John's house from the railway station?
j   I am walking from Ann's house and I want to go to the shops. Do I turn left or right at the police station?

5

Read the following directions showing how to go from John's house to Ann's house. Then write directions showing how to go from Ann's house to John's house. Use these directions to help you and begin as shown.
(From John's house to Ann's house.)
Walk along Park Row to Fir Avenue. Then turn right and walk down Fir Avenue to First Street. Turn left, cross Fir Avenue and walk past the shops to Greenfield Road. Cross Greenfield Road and walk along First Street. Cross North Street and then turn right. Walk past the Ritz Cinema and cross White Avenue. Ann's house is in front of you.

(From Ann's house to John's house.)
Cross White Avenue and walk . . . .
Turn left and then cross . . . .

6

(a)   I am at Ann's house. How can I get to
      i) the school   ii) the market   iii) the railway station?
(Write a few sentences for each set of directions.)

(b)   I am at the main entrance of the factory. How can I get to
      i) the post office   ii) John's house   iii) the main entrance of the library?
(Write a few sentences for each set of directions.)

8 A good idea

1

boat, storm, (strong) wind, weather, (a) sail, shore, idea, shirt, mast;
frightened; far away; instead of; blow, tear, pass, sweep away,
reach, take off, tie, (to) sail, (to) wave; suddenly

2

Dave	This storm is very bad.
Tom	Yes, the sky was blue a few minutes ago.
Dave	The wind's blown the sails down.
Tom	Oh dear. It's sweeping us away from the shore. What can we do?
Dave	I've got an idea. Take off your shirt.
Tom	What are you going to do?
Dave	Watch. We can use our shirts instead of sails.
Tom	What a good idea! I'll put my shirt up, too.
Dave	Now we can reach the shore.

3

Use the sentence table to write two correct sentences about Pictures
1 and 2:

A storm A strong wind	has	blown down swept away	the	sails small boat
One of the boys He		taken off put up	his	shirt clothes

Now write two correct sentences about Picture 3 from the following
table:

A storm A strong wind	has	blown	the	sails small boat	down away
One of the boys He		swept			
		taken	his	shirt clothes	off
		put			up

4

a   What's the weather like in Picture 1?
b   What has the wind done to the sails of the boat?
c   Who is in the boat?
d   What's happened to the storm in Picture 2?
e   Where's the boat?
f   Why can't the boys reach the shore?
g   What has one of the boys done in Picture 3?
h   What's the other boy doing?
i   What's happening in Picture 4?
j   How has the boat reached the shore?

5

Write out the following story. Put one of these words in each blank:

of, off, away, to, near, down, in

(You must use two of the words twice.)

Dave and Tom are sailing _____ a small boat. Suddenly there is
a big storm.
  'The wind's blown the sails _____,' Dave shouts.
  'It's sweeping us _____,' Tom cries. 'What can we do?'
  Dave has got an idea. He and Tom have taken _____ their
shirts. They have tied them _____ the mast _____ their boat,
and now they are using them instead _____ sails. The boat is
sailing _____ the shore and the two boys are waving happily
_____ some people.

6

Now imagine you are Dave. Write this story in a few sentences of
your own.

1

garage, oil cans, tools, cycles, shirts, shorts, pool, lorry; untidy, dirty, clean, shining, smart; (to) clean, (to) oil, greet, (to) cycle, splash, (to) rest

2

Dick   Look. Here are our friends. Their bicycles aren't as clean as ours.

Paul   Yes, they're dirtier than ours.

Dick   But just look at us. We're very dirty now.

Paul   And our friends are cleaner than we are.

Paul   That car's going very quickly. It's splashing our bicycles.

Dick   They're now as dirty as the other bicycles are.

Paul   And we spent so long cleaning them.

Dick   Never mind. Look! This lorry's splashing the others.

Paul   Now their shirts and shorts are as dirty as ours.

Dick   I think they're even dirtier than ours.

3

a   Use these two sentence tables to write six correct sentences about the pictures. (Write at least two sentences from each table.)

Dick's	bicycle shirt	is	dirtier cleaner	than the other boys'	bicycles
Their	bicycles shirts	are	newer smarter		shirts

The other boys'	bicycles	are not	so	dirty clean	as	Dick's	bicycle shirt
	shirts		as	new smart		their	bicycles shirts

b   Now pretend you are Dick. Write two sentences about the big boys' bicycles and clothes.

Your	bicycles clothes	are	better dirtier cleaner older	than	mine his ours theirs

4

a   Where are the two boys in Picture 1?

b   What are they doing?

c   Is the big car as clean as the small one?

d   What are the two boys doing in Picture 2?

e   Are their clothes as clean as the other boys' clothes?

f   Are their bicycles cleaner than the other bicycles?

g   Why are the two boys dirty?

h   What are the boys doing in Picture 3?

i   Why are the big boys laughing?

j   Are the big boys' shirts cleaner than the two boys' shirts in Picture 4? Why not?

5

Write out the story. Put the correct word from the following list in each space.

clean	big	dirty	tidy	untidy
cleaner	bigger	dirtier	tidier	untidier

In Picture 1 Paul and Dick are cleaning their bicycles in a garage. The two bicycles are very_____and the garage is_____.
There are two cars outside the garage: the small car is_____than the large one.

In Picture 2 Paul and Dick are greeting their friends. Their friends are_____than Paul and Dick and their clothes are_____. However, their bicycles are not as_____as Paul's bicycle.
Picture 3 shows the boys on a country road. A car is passing the two boys and splashing their bicycles. Now their two bicycles are as_____as the others. The other boys laugh at them but in Picture 4 a lorry is splashing them. Now their shirts and shorts are even_____than Paul's clothes and Dick's clothes.

6

Now imagine you are Paul and tell this story.

10 How to row a boat

1

rowing-boat, oar, water, lake, father, shorts, cap, shore, rocks, motor-boat; deep, annoyed, proud, high, stuck; (to) row, lose, slip, wave, rescue

2

Mr Black	What are you trying to do, David?
David	I'm trying to reach the shore, of course.
Mr Black	What's the matter?
David	I haven't learnt to row yet.

Peter	Look at that man in the boat. He's rowing towards the rocks.
Alan	Hey, look out . . . He can't hear.
Peter	Oh dear! He's hit the rocks.
Alan	And the boat's stuck on top of them. He isn't able to move.
Peter	Let's call those people in that motor-boat. They'll be able to pull him off the rocks.

3

Use the sentence table to write two correct sentences about the pictures:

David His father The two boys	tried wanted	to	row the boat reach the shore

David Mr Black	could couldn't		row swim to the shore
	was wasn't	able to	get off the rocks rescue his father

4

a What couldn't David do?
b What happened to the oars?
c Where was David's father in Picture 1?
d What did he do in Picture 2?
e Where was he in Picture 3?
f Were there some rocks in front of the boat or behind it?
g What did the two boys try to do?
h Where was the boat in Picture 4?
i What did David's father do?
j Where was the motor-boat going?

5

Read this story carefully.

   David goes in a small rowing-boat on a lake bu_ very well. Soon he loses one of the oars. His father te_ come back to the shore. When David reaches the shore, out of the boat and his father gets in. He wants to show D_ how to row. But he begins to row towards some rocks. Two _ in another boat try to tell him but he does not listen to them. S_ the boat is stuck on the rocks and David's father is not able to ge_ off the rocks. At last a motor-boat pulls him back to the shore.

Now write out the story above. Use 'I' instead of 'David' and make all the necessary changes. Also use the past tense instead of the present tense.

Begin:

   Last week I went in a small rowing-boat on a lake but . . . .

6

Now write this story about David and his father in your own words.

eful books

1

SCHOOL LIBRARY

OUT

2

1

library, shelf, bookcase, photographs, playground, branch, distance;
(to) stamp, borrow, pick, reach

2

Mrs Fish	Look at Jenkins. He's taking a lot of big books.
Mr Short	Is he going to read all of them?
Mrs Fish	He *is* a hard-working boy.
Mr Short	Yes, he's different from the other boys in the school.

Jenkins	Can I borrow these books, sir?
Mr Hill	Yes, of course. Are you going to read all of them?
Jenkins	Yes, sir. I want to improve my English.
Mr Hill	But these books are in Chinese!

3

Use the sentence table to write four correct sentences about the
two pictures:

There are	a lot of	books apples chairs	on the shelves in the library
There is		furniture fruit	on the tree

Now write two correct sentences from the following table:

Jenkins is	borrowing using standing on	the books	to	reach get pick	the apples the fruit

4

a   What's Bob Jenkins doing in Picture 1?
b   What are the two teachers near him doing?
c   What's the other teacher doing?
d   Why are three boys queuing up?
e   How many books are there in the library?
f   What are some boys doing in Picture 2?
g   Are there only a few apples or a lot of apples on the tree?
h   Where's Bob?
i   Who is watching him? Is he surprised or not?
j   What's Bob using the books to do?

5

Bob is taking some large books off a shelf in the school library. One of
the teachers is stamping the books. Bob is carrying the books into
the school playground and is putting them under the branches of an
apple tree. He is standing on the books to reach the apples.

a   Copy the first sentence of the story above. Then write out the
rest of the story, using *going to*. (Example: One of the teachers *is
going to stamp* . . .)
b   Now write out the complete story again, using *has taken*, etc.
(Example: Bob *has taken* some large books off a shelf . . .)

6

Now write this story in your own words.

12 A village

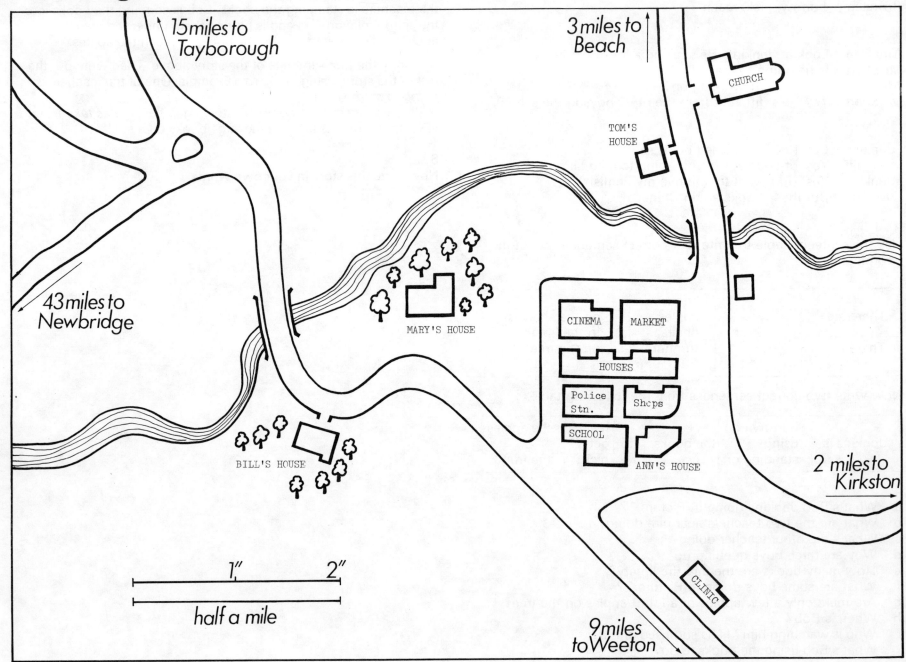

15 miles to Tayborough

3 miles to Beach

CHURCH

TOM'S HOUSE

43 miles to Newbridge

MARY'S HOUSE

CINEMA

MARKET

HOUSES

Police Stn.

Shops

SCHOOL

ANN'S HOUSE

BILL'S HOUSE

2 miles to Kirkston

1"   2"

half a mile

CLINIC

9 miles to Weeton

1

village, country, road, (a) bend, (a) row, river, clinic, church, police station, beach; next to, near, at the side of, beside, in the middle of, opposite, facing, behind, in front of, between, among, across, under, over, round, beyond

2

Tom	Where do you live, Ann?
Ann	Opposite the school. Where do you live?
Tom	We've just moved into the house near the river.
Ann	Is that your house next to those tall trees?
Tom	No, that's Mary's house. I live near the church.
Ann	I know. You live in the old house near the bridge. It's just beyond the market.

Stranger	Where is the police station, please?
Bill	It's in the middle of the village.
Stranger	Do I cross this bridge over the river?
Bill	No, that's the wrong way. Walk up this road and you'll reach a school. The police station is behind the school.

3

Use the sentence table to write six correct sentences about the map:

The police station The church Mary's house	is	in the middle of the village between the shops and the market almost opposite Tom's house
There are some	houses trees	next to Bill's house near the river facing the market

4

a   Who lives near the church?
b   Where does Mary live?
c   Where is the market?
d   Where are the shops?
e   What does Tom pass on his way to the clinic?
f   Which roads cross the river?
g   Which way do I turn if I want to go to the market from Tom's house?
h   What are there round Bill's house?
i   How far is it from the village to the beach?
j   How far is it from Mary's house to the clinic?

5

Write complete sentences from the two lists.
Put each part in List A with the correct part in List B.

A	B
Bill's house is	over the river.
The shops in the village are	on opposite sides of the river.
It is 43 miles	next to the police station.
Mary's house and Tom's house are	beside the cinema.
There are two bridges	to Newbridge.
The market is	opposite Mary's house.

6

a   How can I get from Bill's house to the market?
b   I want to go from Tom's house to the clinic. What will I see on the way?
c   Write a short description of this village.

13 Hit and miss!

1

31

(a) fly, meal, newspaper, something, someone, window; open, hard, happy, surprised, angry; jump up, hit, miss, kill, land (on), cry, clap, appear

2

Mrs Langley	Oh dear. There's a fly near our food.
John	Let me kill it.
Mrs Langley	There isn't anything to hit it with.
John	I'll hit it with an old newspaper.
John	It's landed on something outside the window. I'll hit it now.
Mr Gregg	What are you doing?
John	I'm very sorry, Mr Gregg. I wanted to kill a fly. It landed on something outside the window.
Mr Gregg	Yes, it landed on my head. And you hit my head, but you missed the fly. It's over there now!

3

Use the two sentence tables to write two correct sentences about the pictures:

There was	something	outside the window.	It was	a fly
	someone			
Mrs Langley saw	somebody	near their food.		Mr Gregg

There wasn't	anything	outside the window
	anyone	
John didn't see	anybody	in the room

Now write two correct sentences from the following table:

John	hit	something	with	a stick
Mr and Mrs Langley		Mr Gregg's head		a newspaper
Someone		the fly		his hand

4

a What did Mr and Mrs Langley and their children begin to do?
b Was the table near the window or a long way from it?
c What did the fly do in Picture 1?
d What did John try to do in Picture 2?
e Where did the fly land in Picture 3?
f What did John do?
g What did the others do?

h Who appeared in Picture 4?
i What happened to Mr Gregg? Why was he angry?
j Did John kill the fly?

5

a Each blank in the following sentences shows that one word is missing. Write out the sentences, filling in each blank with the correct word from the list below:

someone	somebody	something
anyone	anybody	anything

(Although it is often possible to use *someone, somebody* and *something* in questions, use only *anyone, anybody* and *anything* in the questions below.)

1 Was there _____ near the food?
   Yes, there was _____ near the food.
   It was a fly.
2 Did John pick _____ up?
   Yes, he picked _____ up.
   It was a newspaper.
3 Was there _____ outside the window?
   Yes, there was _____ outside the window.
   It was Mr Gregg.
4 Did John hit _____ with the newspaper?
   Yes, he hit _____ with it.
   It was Mr Gregg's head.

b Read this story about the pictures:

The Langleys are sitting near a window and having a meal. They cannot eat because there is a big fly. John picks up an old newspaper to kill the fly but he misses it. The fly lands on something outside the window and John hits it with the newspaper. But he does not hit the fly: he hits Mr Gregg's head!

Now write out the story in the past. Begin:

The Langleys were sitting near a window and having a meal. They could not eat because . . . .

6

Now imagine you are John. Write this story in a few sentences of your own.

14 A visit to the doctor

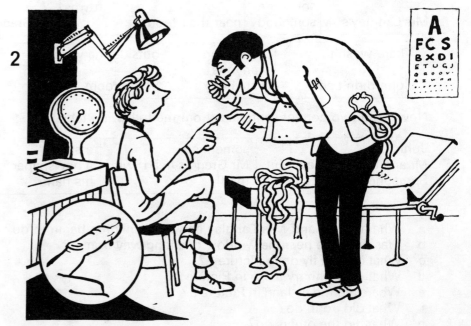

1

doctor, waiting-room, surgery, patients, walking-stick, plaster, bandage, pain, (a) cold, (a) cut, handkerchief, magazine, couch; painful; wait, lean, hurt, knock down, bend over, take off, wear off; hardly

2

Bob Fagg	Hello, Fred. What's wrong?
Fred Watson	A motorbike knocked me down. What's happened to you?
Bob Fagg	I nearly cut my finger off.
Fred Watson	You must be careful.
Dr Lawson	Good evening, Bob. What's the matter?
Bob Fagg	I've cut my finger very badly. It's very painful.
Dr Lawson	Let me take the bandage off.
Bob Fagg	Please don't hurt me.

3

Use the sentence table to write two correct sentences about Picture 1:

The waiting-room Dr Lawson's surgery	is	crowded with full of	sick people patients old men children

Now write two correct sentences about Picture 2 from each of the following tables:

Dr Lawson Bob Fagg Fred Watson The small boy	has	put got	on	his glasses a large bandage
		cut taken	off	his finger his coat

Dr Lawson Bob Fagg Fred Watson The small boy	has	put got	his glasses a large bandage	on
		cut taken	his finger his coat	off

4

a Why are the people waiting in Picture 1?
b Why is the woman using a walking-stick?
c What's the man on the left got on?
d What's the matter with the big boy?
e What's the table full of?
f Where's the big boy in Picture 2?
g What's he doing?
h What's the doctor just done?
i Why is he putting his glasses on?
j What can you see in the small picture?

5

Write out this paragraph. Put one of the following words in each blank:

at   of   off   in   on   round   with

The first picture shows a doctor's waiting-room. It is full_____ people. They are waiting to see the doctor. One boy has his arm _____plaster and he is trying to take_____his coat. A man has a bandage_____his head, a girl is holding a handkerchief _____front_____her nose, and a woman is leaning_____ a walking-stick. A big boy_____a bandage_____his finger is opening the door_____the doctor's surgery.

The second picture shows the boy_____the doctor's surgery. The doctor has just taken the boy's bandage_____and is looking_____his finger. He is putting his glasses_____ because he cannot see the cut_____the end_____the boy's finger. It is so small!

6

Now imagine you are the big boy. Write this story in a few sentences. Begin:

One day I cut my finger with a sharp knife. I put a big bandage on and I went to . . .

15 A visit to a strange planet

1

space, space traveller, people, rocket, Earth, planet, scene, building, square, circle, top, machine, submarine, sky, aeroplane, water, lake, gun; strange, unusual, surprised, friendly; get out of, shine, fly, swim; instead of, like, different

2

Captain Sparks	Look at those two strange people.
Lieutenant Johns	Both have short legs and long arms.
Captain Sparks	Take out your gun. Be careful.
Lieutenant Johns	Look, sir. They want to speak to us.
X	Good day, Captain. Our names are X and Y. What do you want?
Captain Sparks	We want to learn something about you and your people. Why do you speak English?
X	We can speak all Earth languages. Why are you so surprised?
Captain Sparks	Everything is very strange. All the buildings are so tall. Every tree has squares and circles instead of leaves.

3

Write two correct sentences about the picture from each of the following tables. (Write six sentences.)

Both (the)	boys	are very friendly
		have short legs
	strange men	are talking to the space travellers

All	the buildings	are tall
	the trees	have squares and circles
	the machines	are very unusual

Every	building	is tall
	tree	has squares and circles
	machine	
Everything		is very unusual

4

a   Is the planet like the Earth or is it different from the Earth?
b   Where are the space travellers?
c   What are they doing?
d   Are both X and Y attacking the men or are they friendly?
e   What are all the trees like?
f   How many arms have the strange creatures?
g   What is there on top of every building?
h   Where are the strange machines?
i   What are they like?
j   What are both the submarines doing?

5

Read the following description very carefully. It is not a correct description of the picture. Write it out and make it true.

   Six space travellers are getting into their rockets. The planet is full of low buildings: every building is very long and wide. Two strange men are attacking the space travellers. Each man has two short arms and three long legs. He also has three ears and two mouths. All the trees are very strange, too, because they are full of sticks and stones. There are some birds swimming near the trees. There are two submarines in a big lake and an aeroplane in the sky. Everything is very strange.

Begin:

   Four space travellers are getting out of their rockets. The planet is . . .

6

Now write a few sentences of your own about this picture.

35

16 Lost!

1

map, arrow, city, city centre, railway station, library, building, policeman, direction, traffic lights, post office, market, stall, circle; uncertain, lost; on foot; (to) direct

2

Bob	Do you know how to get to Tom's house?
Tina	No, but let's look at this map.
Bob	That's a good idea. The map'll show us where to go.
Tina	Yes. Can you find Clifton Street on it?
Tina	Can you direct me to Clifton Street, please?
Policeman	Go down this street to the traffic lights.
Tina	Yes, I see.
Policeman	Then turn right and take the second turning on your left. It's near there.
Tina	That seems very easy. Thank you very much.

3

Use the sentence table to write a correct sentence about the pictures:

Tina is	asking	some people	the direction
She's		the policeman	the way
Bob and Tina are	telling	someone	the time

Now write two correct sentences from the following table:

Tina	doesn't know	where to go
The policeman	is asking	how to get to Tom's house
Someone	has told them	when to turn left

4

a   Where are Bob and Tina in Picture 1?
b   What are they looking at?
c   What's Tina asking in Picture 2?
d   Why isn't Bob asking the policeman the way?
e   Do they know the way in Picture 3 or are they still uncertain?
f   Are they walking in the same direction or in different directions?
g   What's the boy pointing at?
h   What do you think the girl is going to do?
i   What's the boy doing in Picture 4?
j   Where are they?

5

Look carefully at the second dialogue. Write it out using the verbs *ask* and *tell*.

Example: Tina is asking the policeman to . . . .
He tells her to . . . .
Then he tells her to . . . .

6

Now write this story in a few sentences of your own.

17 'Sorry, sir!'

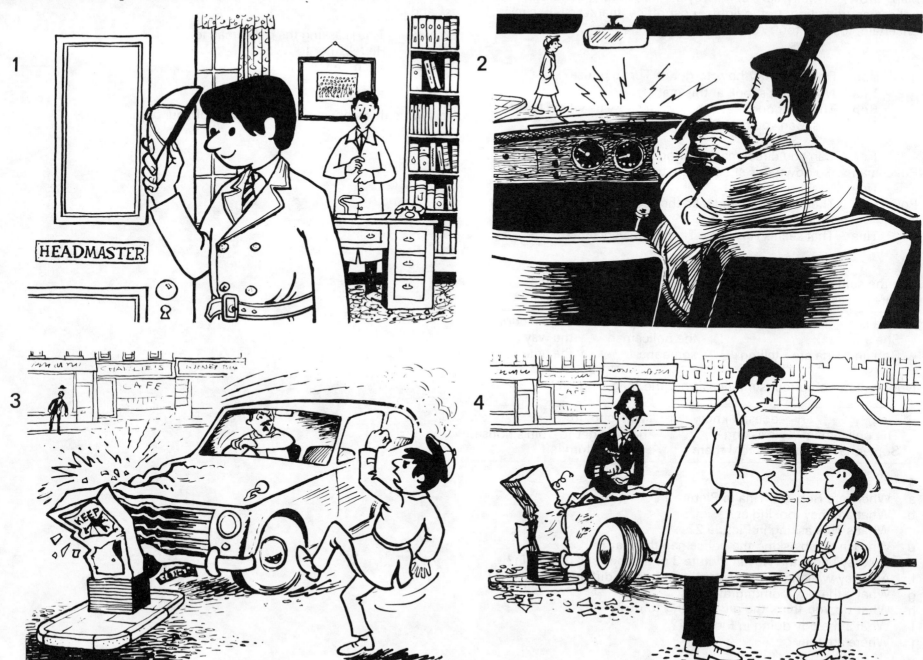

1

office, headmaster, desk, horn, steering-wheel, (a) crossing, fault;
say goodbye, sound (his horn), turn, bump, shake (his fist),
recognise, get out; suddenly, carelessly

2

Tom	It's one minute past four, sir. May I leave now?
Headmaster	Yes, of course. I'm just leaving, too. Have you got a lot of homework?
Tom	Not too much, sir.
Headmaster	Well, I'm going to a concert tonight. You should go out more often. You shouldn't study all the time.
Tom	But my father says I should work hard every night.
Tom	Why are you driving so fast? Couldn't you see me?
Headmaster	You shouldn't run across the road.
Tom	You should drive more carefully. You shouldn't . . . Hello, sir. I didn't recognise you.
Headmaster	Tom, it's you! Are you hurt?
Tom	Oh, no, sir. It was my fault. I'm very sorry.

3

Use the sentence table to write two correct sentences about the
story:

Tom The headmaster	said shouted	'You	should shouldn't	drive more carefully' run across the road' drive in the middle of the road' watch television at home'

Now write two correct sentences from the following table:

The car	which that	Tom saw nearly knocked Tom down stopped	was the headmaster's belonged to the headmaster

4

a   Where was Tom in Picture 1?
b   To whom did he say goodbye?
c   Where was the headmaster in Picture 2?
d   Why did the headmaster sound his horn?
e   What happened to the car in Picture 3?
f   Why did the driver turn?
g   What did Tom do?
h   What did the headmaster do in Picture 4?
i   What did Tom do?
j   Why wasn't Tom angry any longer?

5
Read the story carefully.

Yesterday Tom saw the headmaster. He was very friendly and told Tom to go out more often.

'You shouldn't study all the time,' he said.

Tom left the headmaster's office just after four o'clock and set off home. He started to cross the road near the school. At that moment a big car suddenly came round the corner and almost knocked him over. The car turned and hit a traffic sign. Tom was very angry and shook his fist at the driver.

'You should drive more carefully,' he shouted.

The next moment he recognised the driver of the car. It was the headmaster! The car which nearly knocked him down was the headmaster's.

'Are you hurt?' the headmaster asked Tom.

'No, sir,' Tom answered. 'I'm very sorry. It was all my fault, sir.'

Now imagine that this happened to you. Write out this story, using 'I' instead of 'Tom'.

6
Now imagine you are the headmaster. Write this story in your own words.

1

ladder, bucket, window, ledge, pavement, corner, banana skin, parcel, café, cloud; opposite, sunny; lean, balance, catch (a bus), (to) step, slip, fall down, knock over, (to) land, attack; carelessly

2

Betty	If you aren't careful, you'll fall, Mr Lawson.
Mr Lawson	Well, if I fall, I'll land on top of you.
Betty	Oh dear. That'll be terrible. Be careful.
Mr Lawson	I'll try. But if you don't go away, I will fall.

Betty	Don't cross the road yet, Tony.
Tony	Why not? I can't see any cars.
Betty	No, but I can see a car. If you cross now, the car will knock you down.
Tony	Well, I'll be late if I wait here much longer.
Betty	You've got a lot of time.

3

Use the sentence table to write two correct sentences about the picture:

If the man knocks the bucket over, it falls,	he'll hurt Betty the dog will frighten the boy the boy will run across the road it'll land on Betty

Now write four correct sentences from the following table:

There'll be an accident The girl will fall down The man and woman will get wet The boy will run across the road	if	it rains the boy runs across the road the dog attacks him she walks on the banana skin

4

a   Where's the bucket?
b   What'll happen if it falls?
c   What'll happen if the man up the ladder falls down?
d   What's the girl with the dog doing?
e   What'll happen if the dog escapes?
f   Where's the bus?
g   What'll happen if the girl steps on the banana skin?
h   What'll happen if a car hits the boy on the bicycle?
i   What are the man and woman at the table doing?

j   What'll they do if it begins to rain?

5

Look at the picture and complete each of these sentences:

Example: If the man falls from the ladder, *he'll hurt himself.*
If the bucket falls off the ledge, ...
If the dog escapes, ...
If the boy crosses the road now, ...
The girl will slip if . . . .
The boy will drop all his parcels if . . . .
The man and woman will get wet if . . . .

6

Now describe this picture in a few sentences in your own words. Say what will happen if the man falls down the ladder and if the girl steps on the banana skin, etc.

19 Catching a thief

1

shop window, watch, thief, film, camera, mistake; surprised, brave, angry; approach, (to) notice, break, steal, chase, catch, fight, believe, spoil, laugh

2

Bill	Look, Joe. There's a thief over there.
Joe	He's broken the shop window.
Bill	And he's stealing all the watches.
Joe	Come on! Let's catch him.

Bill	We saw you steal those watches.
'Thief'	You've made a big mistake.
Bill	No, we haven't. *You've* made a mistake.
'Thief'	I'm acting in a film.
Joe	We don't believe you. You're a thief.
'Thief'	Look over there at those cameras. We're making a film. Now you've spoilt it.

3

Use the sentence table to write four correct sentences about the pictures.

A policeman Bill and Joe They No one	saw heard	the man him the two boys them	hit someone break the window run away steal the watches

4

a Where were Bill and Joe in Picture 1?
b What did they hear?
c What did they see?
d What did the man do in Picture 2?
e Why did the boys chase him?
f What happened in Picture 3?
g What did the people in this picture do?
h Why didn't the policeman in Picture 4 help the boys?
i What did he do?
j Why was the man in the chair very angry?

5

One day Bill and Joe are near a shop. There are a lot of watches in the shop window. Suddenly Bill hears a man break the window.
'_____,' Bill cries.

Joe and Bill see the man steal all the watches from the shop window. The thief then turns and runs away.
'_____,' Joe shouts.
The two boys run after the thief. A lot of people look at them but no one helps them. At last they catch the thief and jump on him.
'_____,' Bill says.
'_____,' the man answers.
'_____.'
But Bill and Joe do not believe the man. They see a policeman but he laughs and points to some cameras. The man is not a thief. He really is an actor and he is making a film.

Write out the story and use the past tense. Look at the conversations in Section 2 and write the correct part of the conversation in each blank. Begin:

One day Bill and Joe were near a shop. There were a lot of watches in the shop window. Suddenly Bill heard a man break the window.
'Look, Joe. There's a thief over there,' Bill cried.

6

Now imagine you are Bill. Write this story in your own words.

20 Four journeys

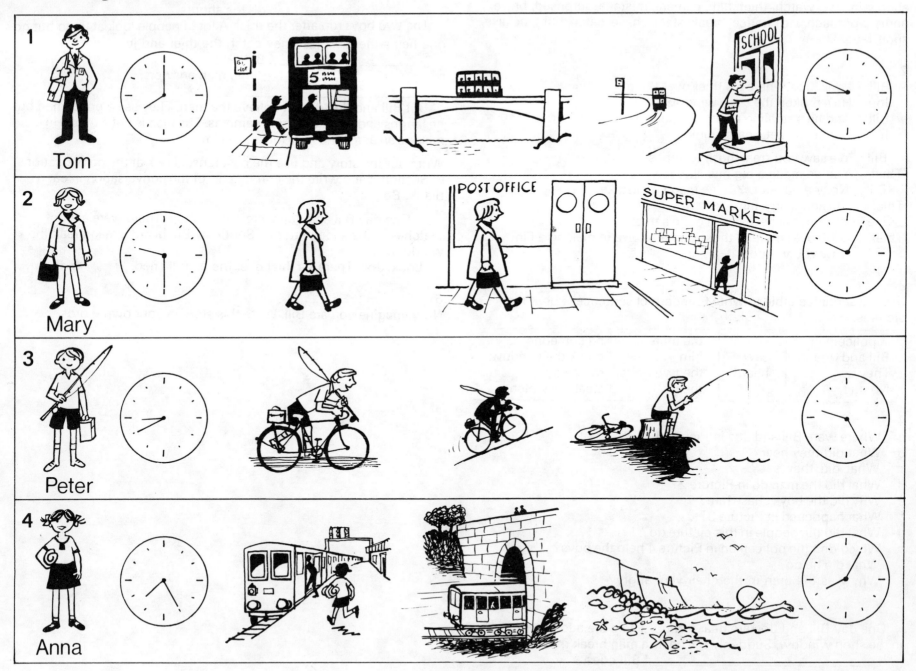

1

way, journey, bridge, school, post office, bicycle, river, train, tunnel; set off, catch, (to) cycle, (to) fish, (to) swim, travel, get to, arrive at, reach; o'clock, (a) quarter past, half past, (a) quarter to, minutes

2

Mary	How long does it take you to get to school, Tom?
Tom	I leave home at eight and arrive at school at ten to nine.
Mary	It takes you fifty minutes—nearly an hour. It's a long time.
Tom	Yes, I go by bus, and it's usually very slow.

Anna	Do you often go fishing?
Peter	Yes, I do. But I have to cycle a long way to the river.
Anna	I go swimming on Sundays and I have to go by train to the beach.
Peter	We'll have to get a car!

3

Use the sentence table to write two correct sentences about the pictures:

It takes	Peter Mary Anna Tom	three quarters of an hour fifty minutes forty minutes over half an hour	to	reach get to	school the shops the river the sea

Now write four correct sentences from the following table:

I We	have to	cycle to the river walk to the shops		
Mary Tom Anna Peter	has to	go to	school the beach	by	train bus

4

a How does Tom travel to school?
b How long does it take Mary to reach the shops?
c What has Peter to cycle over on his way to the river?
d Why does Anna go to the beach?
e What time does Tom set off for school?
f What does Mary pass on her way to the shops?
g How long does it take Tom to reach school?
h How long does it take Anna to get to the beach from her home?

i Who makes the longest journey?
j Who has the shortest journey?

5

It takes *Tom fifty minutes* to get to *school*. He leaves home at *eight o'clock* and arrives at *school* at *ten minutes to nine.* He goes *by bus* and *crosses a big bridge* on the way to *school.*

a Describe Mary's journey in the same way. Use the following in place of the words in italics. (Remember to change *He* to *She.*)
Mary, thirty-five minutes, the shop, half past nine, the shop, five past ten, on foot, passes a post office, the shop
b Now describe Peter's journey in the same way.
c Describe Anna's journey to the beach.

6

Write about your journey to school. What time do you leave home? What time do you arrive at school? How long does it take you? What do you pass on the way to school?

21 An exciting day

1

plant pot, window-sill, (narrow) escape, newspaper, (sports) car, bus stop, (express) train, level-crossing, danger, fire, flames, firemen; interested, interesting, exciting, frightened; almost, nearly, just; wave (goodbye), fall, drop, miss, worry, cross, approach, hit, catch fire

2

Mrs Jones	Goodbye, Peter. Be careful.
Peter	Yes, mother. I'll just finish reading this page.
Mrs Jones	Look out! That plant pot just missed you.
Peter	Good heavens, it nearly killed me. Don't worry. I'll stop reading in a minute.
Alan	Didn't you see that car? It nearly hit you.
Peter	No, I didn't. This story is very exciting.
Alan	Look! That train's going to crash into the bus.
Peter	This story *is* exciting... Why are you frightened?

3

Use the sentence table to write two correct sentences about the pictures:

The plant pot	almost	hits Peter
A sports car	nearly	kills him
The express	just	misses the bus

Now write four correct sentences from the following table:

Peter is reading The people in the bus are frightened The fireman is surprised	when	his mother waves to him the plant pot falls the train nearly crashes into the bus the school catches fire he sees a boy reading

4

a   What's Peter's mother doing in Picture 1?
b   Does the plant pot fall on Peter or does it miss him?
c   Where's Peter going in Picture 2?
d   What does the sports car almost do?
e   Is Peter frightened or not?
f   What's Peter doing in Picture 3?
g   What does the express train do in this picture?
h   What's Peter doing when the school catches fire?
i   What are the other people doing?
j   Does he notice them or not?

5

In Picture 1 Peter is reading when his mother says goodbye to him. He is still reading when a plant pot falls near him.
Now write three pairs of sentences in the same way. Use these words:
Picture 2/read/cross road. Read/sports car/just miss.
Picture 3/read/friend talk to him. Read/train/almost hit bus.
Picture 4/read/classroom catch fire. Read/firemen/arrive.

6

Now write this story in a few sentences of your own.

22 The winner!

1

swimming-trunks, bathing-costume, shorts, clothes, pile, beach, tide, shore, silly, people, idea, race, cross-country race, front, finishing-line; careless, clever; take off, put on, leave, throw, drop, (tides) come in, reach, float, dress, wear, stare, point, cheer

2

Helen	Look at that boy over there.
Dick	Where? I can't see any boys.
Helen	There—at the corner where the new shops are.
Dick	Yes, I can see him now. That's strange. He's wearing swimming-trunks. Hasn't he any clothes to wear?
Helen	I don't know, but he looks silly.
Mr Wise	That big boy's won the race.
Mr Grant	Which big boy?
Mr Wise	He's standing at the roadside near your car.
Mr Grant	I can see him now. Why is he wearing swimming-trunks?
Mr Wise	Perhaps he hasn't any shorts to wear.

3

Use the sentence table to write three correct sentences about the pictures:

Dave The runners	hadn't	any	trousers dry clothes shoes swimming-trunks	to	put on wear
			anything		

Now write three correct sentences from the following table:

The	tide sea water	soon slowly quickly	reached	the spot the place	where	the big rock was Dave's clothes were he left his clothes

4

a Where was Dave in Picture 1?
b Did he put on his clothes or take them off in this picture?
c What was he wearing?
d What did he do in Picture 2?
e Did the tide come in or go out?
f Where were Dave's clothes in Picture 3?

g Why did he walk in the town in his swimming-trunks in Picture 4?
h What did he see in this picture?
i What did he do in Picture 5?
j Why did the people cheer him in Picture 6?

5

Write out this story. Complete each sentence with one of the groups of words at the end of the paragraph.

Yesterday Dave went swimming. He changed into his swimming-trunks near a big rock on the beach and he left his clothes there. Then he went into the sea and began to swim. He did not see _____. Soon the tide reached the big rock _____. When Dave came out of the sea, he _____. They had gone! Poor Dave hadn't _____. He began to walk home but he felt silly _____. Then he saw a cross-country race. Suddenly he had an idea. He joined the race! No one laughed at him then. Everyone cheered when _____.

> anything to wear
> looked for his clothes
> the tide coming in
> because he had his swimming-trunks on
> he crossed the finishing-line
> where his clothes were

6

Now imagine you are Dave. Write this story in a few sentences of your own.

23 The table that got smaller

1

table, table-tennis, (table-tennis) bat, ball, garage, saw, tools, corner, (table) leg; high, difficult, sloping, level, low, impossible; hit, put down, pick up, shorten, (to) saw off, finish, (to) slope

2

Bob	This table is too high. I can't hit the ball.
Peter	We aren't tall enough.
Bob	We're both too small. We can't play table-tennis here.
Peter	Let's shorten the table legs. We can use that saw over there.
Bob	Now the table's sloping.
Peter	We've cut too much off these two legs.
Bob	Oh dear. What can we do now?
Peter	Don't worry. Let's saw some more off the other two legs. Then it'll be level.

3

Use the sentence table to write six correct sentences about the pictures:

Bob Peter	is too	short small stupid		to	reach the table play table-tennis hit the ball
Both boys are Bob is	not	tall big clever	enough		lower the table saw off the legs make the table level

4

a   What did Peter and Bob try to do in Picture 1?
b   Why couldn't they hit the ball?
c   What did Peter do in Picture 2?
d   Where was the saw?
e   What did Peter do in Picture 3?
f   Was the table level or sloping in Picture 4?
g   What was wrong with the table in Picture 5?
h   Did Peter cut any more off the legs?
i   Why couldn't Peter and Bob play on the table in Picture 6?
j   What did the two men do?

5

Write out this story. Join the correct part in List B to the beginning of each sentence in List A.

A	B
One day Peter and Bob began	to cut the table legs.
But they were too small	to play table-tennis.
Peter wanted	shorten the table legs.
So the two boys used a saw to	play table-tennis.
However, the table was not level	to reach the table.
They decided to	enough to play on.
Then the table was too low to	saw off the other legs.

6

Now imagine you are Peter. Write this story in a few sentences of your own.

24 Landslide!

1

fence, bank, railway line, track, express (train), carriage, passenger, tunnel, (storm) clouds, landslide, rock, watch, signal box, signal, signalman, engine driver, bend, danger; wave, pass, appear, leave, shelter, rain (heavily), return, point, approach, warn

2

Tom   Let's tell Mary to hurry. A train's coming.

Ann   Where is she?

Tom   She's just down the road. She's talking to old Mr Jones about the weather.

Jim   She asked me about the weather, too. She thinks it's going to rain!

Ann   The rain's stopped now. Let's walk near the railway line.

Tom   Look! There's been a landslide. That big rock's fallen on to the track.

Ann   Is that a train over there? Let's warn the engine driver about the danger.

Tom   Yes, we'll run and tell the signalman to stop the train at once.

3

Use the sentence table to write four correct sentences about the pictures:

Tom and Ann Ann	talked to spoke to told warned	the signalman the driver him her	about	the danger the landslide the rock on the line the damaged line

Now write four correct sentences from the following table:

Tom The children They	warned asked	the signalman him the driver	to	stop the train be careful change the signal

4

a   What did the children do in Picture 1?

b   Where was the train?

c   Why did all the children run towards the house in Picture 2?

d   Where did they return in Picture 3?

e   What did Mary notice?

f   What did the children do in Picture 4?

g   Where were they in Picture 5?

h   What did they tell the signalman?

i   Why did the train stop in Picture 6?

j   What did the children warn the driver about?

5

Read the following story about four children and a fire. The fire damages a bridge and the children warn a bus driver about it.

Jim, Tom, Ann and Mary are standing near *a bridge*. Mary is talking to *a young lady* a few yards away. They see a *bus* pass by and wave to the passengers. *The sun is shining brightly and it is very hot.* The four children decide to go to a *hut* nearby to shelter from the *sun*. At last *some clouds appear in the sky and the sun is not so bright*. The children begin to return to the *bridge* when Ann suddenly points to something. The *strong sun* has caused a *fire* and it has *burnt* part of the *bridge*.

'There will be a *bus* soon,' Jim cries. 'The driver won't see the danger. Then it will be too late.'

'Let's warn him at once about the danger,' Ann shouts.

Tom, Ann and Mary begin to run up the *road* and disappear round the bend. Jim *stays near the bridge* to tell *any other drivers* about the *fire*.

Soon the *bus* comes and the three children wave their arms and stop it. They tell the driver about the damaged *bridge*.

'Thank you,' the *bus* driver says. 'You have prevented an accident.'

Now write out this story but change the words in italics. In this way you can make your new story describe the pictures. Begin:

Jim, Tom, Ann and Mary are standing near a railway line. Mary is talking to an old man a few yards away . . .

6

Now write this story in your own words. Use the past tense.

25 Waiting for a bus

1

queue, bus stop, lorry, bus conductor, arm, window, clock, country, driver, engine, passenger; full, steep, tired; (to) queue, splash, pass, come, get on, push (in front of), hold out, look out for, travel, stop, break down, try, mend, wave

2

Dick Large	We can't all get on this bus. Get out of our way.
Bobby Small	But we were in the queue before you.
Dick Large	We don't care. You'll have to wait for another bus.
Bobby Small	Please let us get on the bus. We have to visit a friend in hospital.
Dick Large	You can visit him tomorrow!
Bobby	Look! There's the other bus. It's stopped up that hill.
Charles	We're going to pass it.
Bobby	Can you see those four boys?
Charles	Ha, ha! They'll have to wait a long time now. Their bus has broken down.
Bobby	Let's wave to them.

3

Use the sentence table to write four correct sentences about the pictures:

All the people The three small boys Bobby Small Dick Large The driver	had to	wait for another bus stand in the queue visit a friend in hospital wait a long time in the bus change the wheel

4

a   Where were the three small boys in Picture 1?
b   Where were the four big boys?
c   Why did the people in the queue get wet?
d   What did the four big boys do in Picture 2?
e   Why did the conductor hold out his arm in Picture 3?
f   What had the three small boys to do?
g   How long had they to wait for the next bus?
h   Where was the bus in Picture 5?
i   What happened to the number 26 bus?
j   What did the three small boys do in Picture 6?

5

Write out the story. Choose the best word or phrase from the words in the brackets.

One day three small boys called Bobby, Charles and Peter went to visit their friend (in a hospital, in hospital, in the hospital). They waited (a long time, long, long ago) for a bus. When the bus (arrived, reached, came to), it was nearly full. Suddenly four big boys pushed (at the side of, among, in front of) them and got (in, on, at) the bus.

'We were in the (line, row, queue) before you,' Bobby shouted.

'We don't care,' one of the big boys answered. 'You'll have to wait for another bus.'

After (an hour, half an hour, an hour and a half), the (next, near, after) bus came and the three boys got on. (On, In, During) their way (to hospital, to the hospital, to a hospital), they saw the first bus (at the bottom of, half-way up, at the top of) a hill in front of them.

'It's (broken off, broken up, broken down),' Charles cried.

'Now those four boys will have to wait a long time for another bus,' Bobby laughed.

6

Now write this story in your own words. Imagine that you are one of the small boys. Instead of 'he' and 'they', use 'I' and 'we', etc.

26 A surprise

1

airport, Indian, porter, case, basket, (dark) glasses, care, arm, policeman, whistle, corner, woods, surprise, fright, snake, lid; large, huge; quietly, carefully, quickly; arrive, pick up, steal, follow, blow (a whistle), drive, open, appear

2

Dave X	Look at that man with the big basket. He seems very rich.
Mr Y	If *you* talk to him, *I'll* steal the basket.
Dave X	That's a good idea. There's probably a lot of money in it.
Mr Y	Be careful. There's a policeman with a whistle over there.
Mr Raj	Stop, thief! Stop, thief!
Policeman	What's happened, sir?
Mr Raj	That man with the dark glasses and that boy are thieves. They've just stolen my basket.
Policeman	We'll catch them, sir. What was there in the basket?
Mr Raj	A snake!

3

Use the sentence table to write six correct sentences about the pictures:

An Indian	with	a basket	arrived at the airport
The boy and the man		some cases	was talking to someone
A policeman		dark glasses	drove quickly away
		a snake	had a big surprise
		a whistle	tried to stop the thieves

4

a What was the Indian doing in Picture 1?
b Who was watching him?
c Who spoke to the Indian in Picture 2?
d What did the man do?
e What did the man and the boy do in Picture 3?
f What did the policeman do in Picture 4?
g Where did the man and the boy go in this picture?
h What did the car pass in Picture 5?
i Where were the man and the boy in Picture 6?
j Why were they surprised and frightened?

5

Write out the story and complete each sentence with one of the groups of words at the end of the paragraph.

One day an Indian with _____ arrived at an airport. It was too heavy to _____, so he put it down and began to look for a porter. Just then he noticed _____. The boy came up to him and _____. At the same time, a man with _____ picked up his basket. Then the man and the boy ran away. The Indian hurried to a policeman with _____ and _____. But it was no use. The boy and the man got into a car and _____.

The car passed _____ and then went towards _____. When it reached the wood, _____ and the man and the boy got out. They opened the basket and, to their great surprise, _____.

a small boy, it stopped, a zoo, carry, a whistle, a basket, they saw a snake, drove off, a wood, dark glasses, tried to stop the thieves, began to talk to him

6

Now write this story in your own words. Imagine you are the boy.

27 The chase

1

parcel, moon, stars, footpath, smoke, chimney, direction, bridge, river, something; parked, dark, windy, alone, distant, lonely, close(r), relieved; get off, hurry, blow, turn round, chase, catch up with, hold, attack, drop

2

Stranger	You *do* walk quickly. It's taken me a long time to catch up with you.
John	What do you want? Why have you followed me?
Stranger	I've hurried after you to give you this parcel.
John	What's inside it? It isn't . . .
Stranger	It's yours. You dropped it.
John	Oh dear! I never noticed.
Stranger	I know. I've had to run a long way to return it to you.

3

Use the sentence table to write four correct sentences about the pictures:

	ran after John		tell him about the parcel
Someone	followed him		give him something
The man behind	hurried after him	to	attack him
	ran a long way		steal the parcels

Now write two correct sentences from the following table:

	the man	a long time		catch up with him
It took			to	
	him	a quarter of an hour		stop John

4

a   What did John do in Picture 1?
b   Describe the scene in a sentence.
c   Where was John hurrying in Picture 2?
d   Was he alone or was someone following him?
e   Why was he frightened in Picture 3?
f   What did he begin to do in Picture 4?
g   What was the man doing?
h   What did the man do in Picture 5?
i   What did he do in Picture 6?
j   Why did he follow John?

5

One day last week I went shopping. It took me a long time to do all my shopping and I caught a bus home late in the evening. It was very dark when I got off the bus. I had to walk home through a lonely wood and I felt a little frightened. Suddenly I heard a noise. There was a strange man behind me. I began to run home very quickly and the man behind me began to run very quickly, too. Then I crossed a bridge over the river and saw my house a long way off. The next moment the man caught me and held my arm.

'I followed you to give you this parcel,' he said.

I was very surprised and very glad, too.

'Thank you very much,' I laughed. 'You are very kind.'

Write out this story. Change 'I' to 'John' or 'he', etc. Begin:

One day last week John went shopping . . .

6

Now write this story in a few sentences of your own. This time imagine you are the man.

28 A cry for help

1

cliff, ledge, help, beach, climber, boat, ship, nest, bird; narrow, steep, angry, frightened, hurt; lie, shout, climb up, reach, rescue, jump up, pretend, slip, fall, (not) take any notice; angrily

2

Charlie Brown	Look up there! There's a boy lying on that narrow ledge.
Timothy West	Where? I can't see anyone.
Charlie Brown	He's half-way up the cliff.
Timothy West	Yes. I can see him now. Let's climb up there at once.
Charlie	We've almost reached you. Don't worry.
Peter	You'll never get me off this ledge.
Charlie	There are three other climbers coming up behind me. It won't be hard.
Peter	You've all come to help me! Look, I'm not hurt. It's just a joke!

3

Use the sentence table to write six correct sentences about the pictures:

There	is	a boy a climber someone	walking on the beach lying on a narrow ledge shouting for help
	are	four men some climbers a lot of people	climbing up the cliff coming to rescue him watching the rescue

4

a   Where was the boy in Picture 1?
b   What was he doing?
c   Where were the four men?
d   What did they do in Picture 2?
e   What did the boy do in Picture 3?
f   Where was he in Picture 4?
g   What happened in Picture 5?
h   What did he do in Picture 6?
i   Was he really hurt or not?
j   What did the four men on the beach do?

5

Read the following story about a shepherd boy (a boy who looks after sheep) and a wolf.

One day there was a boy *looking after some sheep*. Suddenly he *stood up* and began to cry *'Wolf! Wolf!'* The people *in the nearby village* heard him and *ran across the field* to help him. But when they reached the boy, he *sat down* and laughed at them.

'It's just a joke!' he cried. *'There's no wolf attacking the sheep.'*

The *villagers* were angry with him and returned to *their village*. A few moments later they heard the boy shout again. This time, however, *there really was a wolf killing the sheep*. But *the villagers* did not take any notice of the boy.

'It's just another joke!' they said angrily.

Now write out this story but change the words in italics. In this way you can make your new story describe the pictures.

6

Now write this story in your own words. Imagine you are the boy.

Appendix

1 Grammatical and structural items

1 *There is . . . /There are . . .*

There is a train in the station.
There are some buses outside the entrance.
Present Continuous; singular and plural
A man is hurrying past the ticket collector.
Some people are drinking tea.

2 Adjectives

Bill is throwing away an old shoe.
The man is angry with Toby.

3 Present Simple: *want/need/like*

Bill wants a holiday on a quiet beach.
They all need a holiday near the sea.
Bill Short doesn't like a lot of noise.
Bill and Alan don't like crowded beaches.

4 *Going to*

Ted Smart is going to pass the lorry.

5 Sentences containing *because*

Why is Peter painting the room? Because he wants to help his
   father.
Mrs Green is happy because Mr Green and Peter are painting
   the room.

6 Present Perfect and *just/already*

Leela has just paid for the ice cream.
The children have already gone to the new shop.

7 Imperatives

Go straight on at the crossroads.

Prepositional phrases

The post office is on the left.

8 Verb + participle

A storm has blown down the sails.
A strong wind has swept the small boat away.

9 Comparison of adjectives

Dick's bicycle is cleaner than the other boys' bicycles.
Their shirts are not so dirty as Dick's shirt.

Possessive pronouns

Your bicycles are better than ours.

10 *Try/want to do something*

David tried to reach the shore.
His father wanted to row the boat.

Could(n't)/Was(n't) able to

He couldn't swim to the shore.
Mr Black wasn't able to get off the rocks.

11 *A lot of* + count/non count nouns

There are a lot of books on the shelves.
There is a lot of furniture in the library.

Sentences showing purpose: *to* + infinitive

Jenkins is using the books to reach the apples.

12 Prepositional phrases

The police station is in the middle of the village.
The church is next to Bill's house.
There are some houses opposite the shops.

13 *Something/Someone/Somebody/Anything/Anyone/Anybody*

There was something outside the window.
John didn't see anyone in the room.

Do something *with* something

John hit the fly with a newspaper.

14 Adjective + preposition

The waiting-room is crowded with sick people.

Verb + participle

Dr Lawson has put on his glasses.
The small boy has taken his coat off.

15 *Both/All/Every*

Both the men are very friendly.
All the buildings are tall.
Every tree has squares and circles.
Everything is very unusual.

16 *Ask/Tell/Know + where to/how to/when to*

Tina doesn't know where to go.
She's asking how to get to Bob's house.
Someone has told them when to turn left.

17 *Should/Shouldn't*

Tom said, 'You should drive more carefully.'

Clauses with *which/that*

The car which Tom saw was the headmaster's.
The other car that stopped belonged to the head.

18 Sentences containing *if*

If the man knocks the bucket over, he'll hurt the woman.
There'll be an accident if it rains.

19 *See/Hear* someone do something

A policeman saw the man hit someone.
No one heard him break the window.

20 *It takes . . . to . . .*

It takes Tom fifty minutes to get to school.
Has to

Peter has to cycle to the river.

21 Position of adverbs

The plant pot almost hits Peter.

Sentences containing *when*

Peter is reading when the plant pot falls.
The fireman is surprised when he sees a boy reading.

22 Adjectival phrases following nouns

Dave hadn't any dry clothes to wear.

Sentences containing *where* (adjectival clauses)

The tide soon reached the place where he left his clothes.

23 *. . . too short to . . . / . . . not tall enough to . . .*

Bob is too short to reach the table.
He is not tall enough to hit the ball.

24 *Talk to/Speak to: tell/warn*

Tom and Ann spoke to the driver about the landslide.
They warned him about the danger.

Ask someone to do something

Tom asked the signalman to stop the train.

25 *Had to* do something

All the people had to wait for another bus.

26 Adjectival phrases: *with*

A policeman with a whistle tried to stop the thieves.

27 Infinitive of purpose

Someone ran after John to tell him about the parcel.

It took . . . to . . .

It took him a long time to stop John.

28 *There is* + noun + *ing* form of verb

There is a boy lying on a narrow ledge.
There are four men climbing up the cliff.

2 Helpful phrases for describing pictures

in the foreground
in the background
in the distance
in the middle-distance
in the middle
at/in the centre
on the horizon
in sight
out of sight
on the left
on the right
on the left-hand side
on the right-hand side
in the top left-hand corner
in the bottom left-hand corner
in the top right-hand corner
in the bottom right-hand corner
at the top (of the picture)
at the bottom (of the picture)